My Geeky Sister Saves the Day

By Pamela Rushby
Illustrated by Tomso

Pearson Australia
(a division of Pearson Australia Group Pty Ltd)
707 Collins Street, Melbourne, Victoria 3008
PO Box 23360, Melbourne, Victoria 8012
www.pearson.com.au

First published 2014 by Pearson Australia
2021 2020 2019 2018
10 9 8 7 6 5 4 3 2 1

Publisher: Kieren Noonan
Project Managers: Tamara Pirois and Rachel Davis
Lead Editors: Kerry Nagle and Beth Zeme
Editor: Philip Bryan
Cover and Series Designers: Jenny Grigg and Anne Donald
Designers: Nina Heryanto and Leigh Ashforth
Copyright & Pictures Editor: Katy Murenu
Mac Operator: Rob Curulli
Cover art: Tomso
Illustrator: Tomso
Printed in Australia by the SOS Print + Media Group

ISBN 978 1 4860 0759 2

Pearson Australia Group Pty Ltd ABN 40 004 245 943

Acknowledgements
Every effort has been made to trace and acknowledge copyright. However, if any infringement has occurred, the publishers tender their apologies and invite the copyright holders to contact them.

Disclaimer
Some of the images used in *My Geeky Sister Saves the Day* might have associations with deceased Indigenous Australians. Please be aware that these images might cause sadness or distress in Aboriginal or Torres Strait Islander communities.

Contents

Chapter 1

Bonnie is an alien

Sometimes I think my sister Bonnie is an alien. That the real Bonnie must have been abducted and a copy left in her place.

It's not that Bonnie looks like an alien. There's none of the two-heads, or three-eyes or tentacles-instead-of-arms thing going on. Bonnie looks pretty normal, for an older sister: long brown hair, brown eyes, that sort of thing. In fact, she looks a lot like the rest of us, Mum, Dad, my older brother Elliot and me – I'm Xander – because we've all got brown hair and brown eyes, too.

No, it's not how Bonnie looks that makes her totally different from the rest of us. It's what she's interested in.

The rest of us are musos. Mum and Dad are folkies, they play fiddle and bodhran and flute in a group with some other people. They call themselves Paddy's Pigs, so you can guess what they play. That's right, Irish music. They hang out at a folk club in town, with other folkies with weird names, like Blokes in Skirts (that's two guys who play bagpipes), and The Tiddly Poms (English folk music), and Ned and the Kellys (Australian folk music), and The Awkward Orchestra (that's when they all play together).

My brother Elliot's 15, and he's into electronic music. He's put together his own DJ equipment, and he's mixing and scratching away half the night. Sometimes it even sounds all right.

I like guitar. Unplugged acoustic guitar, that is – not electric. I'm kind of into music like Willie Nelson, Bob Marley, Pink Floyd, the Beatles, Led Zeppelin, Sting, Eric Clapton. If you haven't heard them, you haven't heard real guitar. Check them out.

So, with the rest of the family like that, you'd think Bonnie would like music. Well, she doesn't *dislike* it. But what she really loves is … science.

Bonnie loves to know why things are so, and how things work, and what makes them go. She watches documentaries and she reads books, and she loves those guys on television who are always testing out science myths to see if they're real.

"Look at this!" she'll shriek with delight. "Come and watch! They're going to try to find out if a person with a tongue piercing is more likely to be struck by lightning!"

Or, "Oh my gosh! Today the program's about whether an aeroplane toilet can create enough suction to cause a person to become stuck on it!"

Or, "Would you believe it? They're going to see if a scuba diver can be sucked up by a firefighting helicopter!"

Bonnie likes to pull things apart to see how they work, too. Clocks, radios, little clockwork toys, Mum's hairdryer. Sometimes she even manages to put them back together again.

So, what's wrong with that, you're asking? Everyone's different. Everyone's interested in different things. Nothing wrong with it at all, really. I just always thought Bonnie was kind of weird. A geek. A nerd. Until … until the time one of my geeky sister's science experiments saved our street.

Let me tell you about our street. It's out of town a bit, you have to go down a long road from the middle of our little town, and across a bridge over the creek, and down the road again and turn left, and you're in our street. There are only half a dozen houses, each with a largish garden. Our house is the only one with kids. The other houses are owned by oldish people, who moved here to retire and grow veggies and keep chooks. Mr Harper keeps bees. Mrs Adamcyk makes the best jam drops and Anzac biscuits. Mr Singh paints – pictures, I mean, not houses – and Mrs Singh cooks fantastic curries.

Mrs Wong does tai chi on her verandah every morning. You have to be careful going past, or she'll call you to join in and you'll have to "stroke the monkey", or do "white crane spreads wings" with her for hours.

Mr Bartlett – Ted, he likes to be called – has a huge shed full of old stuff that he tinkers with all the time. If anyone needs a nail, bolt, or a bit of wire, or a piece of wood, they know they'll find it in Ted's shed.

Our street, in fact, is a very interesting place to live. We get cut off from town every so often, if it rains a lot and the creek comes up and floods the bridge, but we're used to that. It's not a huge problem.

But I was telling you about Bonnie. It was her birthday not long ago, it comes about a month before Christmas, and she was 12. She had some friends around after school for pizza and ice cream, and they brought Bonnie presents like sparkly nail polish, smelly shower gels, glittery things to put in her hair, CDs of boy bands.

"Thanks!" Bonnie said. "I love them!"

Then the girls asked, "What did your family give you?"

Well, of course we'd all known what Bonnie would really like. Mum and Dad got her a couple of kits, so she could build things and make them work. Elliot got her a book he thought she'd like to read, *The Boy Who Harnessed the Wind.* And I got her another book, which I'd found on the Internet and ordered especially, *Cool Science Experiments for Kids.* I'd flipped through it, and there were dozens, absolutely dozens, of experiments to try that would keep her going for a while.

SCIENCE
MUSIC
ROCK
hello
12
Ho

The girls were seriously *not* impressed. They smiled and said, "Isn't that great?" but there was a lot of eye-rolling when Bonnie wasn't looking, and you could see they thought that, as a family, we were 'not good at presents'.

Chapter 2

Bonnie's idea of fun

But we were 'good at presents'. Bonnie loved her presents. She was into the book I'd given her the next weekend. And the weekend after that. And the one after that. I was waiting for my friends Jase and Tommo to come over and play my new computer game, Dragons of Doom. I watched as Bonnie searched the house for glass jars and string and old newspapers and plastic bottles, and took over a lot of space on the deck to put them together in strange and mysterious ways. What had I started when I gave her that book?

SOCKS

"What are you making?" I asked. "You've taken Socks' dish." Socks is our cat. He's very attached to his food dish. It has his name on it. Bonnie was going by with an armful of old glass jars, a ball of wool and a box of baking soda – and Socks' dish.

"It's just the right size," Bonnie said, looking at the dish. "I'll give it back."

"But what are you making?" I asked again.

"Stalactites and stalagmites," said Bonnie, in one of those tones older sisters use that mean, *Don't you even know that*?

I went to find Socks another dish. If I knew Bonnie's projects, giving it back didn't necessarily mean anytime soon.

Jase and Tommo arrived. "Let's go!" I said. "I'm up to Level 3!" But Jase and Tommo were more interested in what Bonnie was doing.

She'd poured hot water into the two glass jars, spooned baking soda into them, then stirred and stirred. When it had all dissolved, she put more baking soda in and stirred again.

SOCKS

"Why are you doing that?" Jase asked.

"I need to dissolve as much baking soda as I can into each jar," Bonnie said.

"Um, right," said Tommo. "And then?"

"Then I loop the wool between them."

"Can we watch?" asked Jase.

"Sure," said Bonnie. She glanced at me. "Admit it," she said. "You're interested. You have to be."

She was right. I was interested. I watched as Bonnie twirled strands of wool together. She weighted the ends by tying them onto old metal nuts. "I got these from Ted's shed," she said. She dropped the nuts into the jars, so the wool was partly in the baking-soda solution. She arranged the rest of the wool in a loose loop, hanging above the saucer.

"Now what?" I asked.

"That's it. Done."

"But what's going to happen?" Tommo wanted to know. By the look on his face, he'd forgotten all about Dragons of Doom.

Bonnie picked up *Cool Science Experiments for Kids* and showed us the page she was working from. "If it all works as it should, the solution in the jars soaks into the wool and creeps along it until it reaches the lowest point of the loop. Right there, see, above Socks' dish. Then it should drip down onto the dish."

"And?"

"And make stalactites and stalagmites."

"How long's that going to take?"

Bonnie checked the book again. "Oh. A few days."

A few days! I was glad I'd found Socks another dish.

"Are you sure it's going to work?" I asked.

"Well, no," said Bonnie. "You can't ever be sure. But it'll be interesting to find out!"

And you know what? It did work! In a couple of days the solution had started to drip from the middle of the wool. It solidified and hung down from the wool. That was the stalactite, Bonnie said. The little pile forming on Socks' dish, growing upwards, was the stalagmite. "They should meet in the middle and form a column, in a while," Bonnie said.

They didn't, though. Not because the experiment failed, but because Socks jumped up onto the table and knocked one of the jars over. Maybe he wanted his dish back.

Chapter 3

Our front yard erupts

Bonnie's next project was a volcano. Socks got to keep his dish this time; what Bonnie needed was a plastic soft-drink bottle, wallpaper paste and lots of newspaper. To make the volcano erupt, she needed detergent, vinegar and more baking soda. (Mum couldn't understand how fast the baking soda was disappearing at our house; it was on the supermarket shopping list every week.) Oh, and a bit of red food colouring.

I helped Bonnie make the volcano, just because it was messy and fun.

We had to cut the screw-on bit off the bottle, and then tape the bottle firmly, standing up, onto a big piece of wood for a base. (The wood came from Ted's shed.)

We scrunched up balls of newspaper and taped them to the bottle, wider at the bottom and getting narrower and narrower as we went up, leaving the top of the bottle open.

Then we got on to the fun bit. We tore strips of newspaper, dipped them into the wallpaper paste and stuck them, layer upon layer, all over the newspaper balls until we had a smoothish surface. We shaped it like a cone, well, like a volcano, actually.

We had to leave it to dry for a few days, then we could paint it to look like a real volcano, brown and black. I wanted to paint streams of red and orange lava flowing down the sides, but Bonnie said no. She said we were going to do that for real.

"Are we?" I said. "Can I call Jase and Tommo to come over?"

"Sure," said Bonnie.

It didn't take them long to get there.

"What's it going to do?" asked Jase.

"Oh, just erupt," said Bonnie.

Jase and Tommo took a step back.

Bonnie checked her book. Then she got some warm water and poured it into the bottle until it was almost full.

"You can put the red food colouring in if you like," she said to me.

"What'll that do?"

"We'll get red lava."

Red lava! Cool! I put the colour in.

Then I had a thought. "Is this going to bubble over? Go everywhere? Mum won't like it if it goes all over the deck. Maybe we'd better take it out to the yard."

"Good thinking," Bonnie said. "I don't quite know how it'll react." So we carefully carried the volcano into the front yard.

Mum, Dad, Elliot and a few of the neighbours stopped to watch.

"What's going on?" asked Mr Harper.

"It's a volcano!" I told him. "It's going to erupt!"

"Erupt?" said Mrs Singh nervously. "Do you mean explode?"

"No, no," said Bonnie. "It won't explode. At least I don't think so."

"That's a bit of my wood it's sitting on," Ted announced proudly.

"Ready?" Bonnie said. "Here goes."

Everyone moved back a little.

Bonnie added a little detergent to the bottle. She poured in two tablespoons of baking soda.

"So *that's* where all the baking soda's been going!" said Mum.

Bonnie slowly poured in some vinegar.

She stepped back. Nothing happened for a second. Then red bubbles poured out of the bottle and cascaded down the sides of our volcano. They spread over the base and across the grass.

"Eruption!" I shouted.

Bonnie stood with a big grin. Everyone cheered and clapped.

"But why does it do that?" Mrs Wong asked.

"The baking soda reacts with the vinegar," explained Bonnie. "It produces carbon dioxide. The detergent just makes bubbles and forces its way out to make the lava."

Our neighbours were all very impressed with Bonnie's experiment. Unfortunately, they weren't nearly as impressed with her next one.

Chapter 4

Off the scale

What Bonnie was interested in finding out next, from *Cool Science Experiments for Kids*, was whether stress can affect body temperature. The idea was to put people in a stressful situation and take their temperature before and after, to see whether it had risen.

"What's the problem?" Elliot said. "There's plenty of stressful situations in this house!"

"It has to be the same stressful situation," Bonnie read from her book. "And there's only five of us. I need about ten subjects to test it properly."

"Ask the neighbours," I suggested. "They probably wouldn't mind helping. They loved your volcano."

So Bonnie went door to door, and the neighbours said they'd be happy to help.

"Does everyone need to do it at the same time?" Mum asked.

Bonnie checked her book. "It doesn't say so," she said.

"Well, why don't we do that anyway?" said Mum. "We can make an occasion of it; give everyone afternoon tea for helping, and we'll all do it together."

Bonnie had some preparation to do first. She had to produce a stressful situation. *Cool Science Experiments for Kids* suggested a test of mental arithmetic problems, with lots of questions, that had to be done in a set time.

Elliot looked at the test Bonnie worked out. "These are too easy. Let's add a few more," he said, grinning. "Really really tricky ones. That'll get them going!"

On Sunday afternoon, all the neighbours gathered on our deck. I'd meant to go and play soccer with some of my mates, but when I saw that afternoon tea I changed my mind. Mum had made tea and home-made lemonade, plus scones and cakes. There was a big pavlova, oozing cream and fruit, that she said she was keeping for after we'd all done the test.

Having afternoon tea first was all part of the plan, because Bonnie wanted her subjects to relax. "Now," she said, "could you rate your current stress level on a scale of 1–10, please?"

After that afternoon tea, no-one was feeling stressed. In fact, some of them looked as if they might drift right off to sleep.

"I need to take your temperatures now," Bonnie said. "And I'll make a note of it." She got Mum to help her. They'd borrowed as many thermometers as they could.

Then, Bonnie handed out the tests, and pencils. "You have only five minutes to complete the whole test," she said sternly.

"Anyone who doesn't complete it doesn't get a piece of pavlova."

She looked around. "Are you ready? Go!"

Pencils scribbled. Fingers flew. Foreheads crinkled in concentration. There were cries of anguish as people made mistakes. You could almost hear the air sizzle. It was sizzling around me, all right. I couldn't do half these sums in my head. And I love pavlova!

"Time!" announced Bonnie. Immediately, there were protests.

"I'm not finished!"

"These are really hard!"

"Extra time! Extra time!"

Bonnie wouldn't give anyone extra time. She took everyone's temperature again, and noted it down. Then she wanted to know how stressed they felt now, on the scale of 1–10.

"Off the scale", almost everyone said. Absolutely off the scale.

"I agree," said Elliot. "And I didn't even do the test!"

Except Ted, who was a whiz at mental arithmetic. He'd finished the whole test with time to spare, and was happily reading *Cool Science Experiments for Kids*. "I can't imagine what all the fuss is about," he said. "Now, where's my pavlova?"

Most of the neighbours didn't want any pavlova. They said they felt too stressed and upset to eat it. They got up and staggered off home.

"Shattered," muttered Mrs Wong. "I'm just shattered. I need to go and do some tai chi to settle my nerves."

"Think I'll go and talk to my bees for a bit. That always calms me down," said Mr Harper. "Bonnie, that was even worse than primary school!"

"So what was the result?" I asked Bonnie.

"Definite increases in body temperature," she said. She showed me her notes.

"Wow," I said. "Lucky there weren't any heart attacks."

That concerned Mum. “Bonnie,” she said, “I think your next project should be something rather … low key.”

Even Bonnie had been a bit startled by the neighbours’ reactions to her stress test. She was staring across the street, watching Mrs Wong as she practised “cloud hands” on her verandah. Mrs Wong still looked rather shaky.

“Um, yes,” Bonnie said. “Maybe I’ll make up one of my birthday kits. Or maybe I’ll start reading my book about the boy who harnessed the wind.”

“I think that’s a really good idea,” said Mum.

Chapter 5

Making electricity

The birthday kit Bonnie started making up was in a box labelled Power Up! It had a picture of a small windmill on it.

"What's it do?" I asked.

Bonnie was studying the instructions carefully. "It makes electricity," she said. "You build this little windmill and when the wind spins it, it makes electricity."

"Really?" I said. "How's it do that?"

"The same way big wind farms do," said Bonnie. "The blades on a windmill are driven by the wind, and that spins a shaft that connects to a generator and makes electricity. Basically, the windmill converts wind energy. It's all about transferring energy from one medium into another."

I stared at her. "Oh, right," I said. "I thought it might be something like that."

Bonnie sighed. "Think of it like this. Think of a boat with a sail, a yacht. The wind – moving air – pushes on the sail and that makes the boat move. The wind's transferred its energy to the boat. Got that?"

"Yeah," I said. "I can just about work that one out."

"Well, if you put a windmill blade in that wind, and the wind's energy makes the blade turn, you're transferring energy again. Only it's more complicated when you're making electricity, because you're using that energy to spin a shaft that leads into a generator. And the generator turns that energy into electricity."

I tried hard to look intelligent. I could picture the parts, but I couldn't fit them together.

Power up!

"Couldn't have explained it better myself, Bonnie," someone said. Ted was coming up the stairs to the deck.

"But … " I said. "But …"

"But *what*?"

"But *how* does the generator do that?"

"Well." Bonnie looked at her instructions again. "The generator has a conductor in it, a coiled wire, and that's surrounded by magnets. The shaft, as it rotates, turns the magnets around the conductor and that generates an electric current."

"Yup," I said. "Clear as mud,"

"It's the same way the dynamo on your bike works," Ted said. "Only on your bike, you're supplying the energy, by pedalling. And that energy turns the wheels."

"Uh," I said. I was still trying to look intelligent.

"That's funny you should mention a bike," Bonnie said to Ted.

"And why's that?"

"Well, the book I've been reading is about a boy who made electricity using a windmill and parts of an old bike," said Bonnie. She picked up her birthday book, *The Boy Who Harnessed the Wind*, and handed it to Ted. "His name's William Kamkwamba and he's from Malawi, in Africa. He built a windmill out of old junk and he made enough electricity to put lights into his family's house."

"Why'd he want to do that?" Mum asked. "Fed up with the power bill?" Mum and Dad and Elliot had come out onto the deck. Dad had an armful of recyclable shopping bags.

"No, it was because they didn't have electricity at all," Bonnie explained. "No one in their village did. He wanted to be able to read at night, instead of just going to bed when it got dark."

"You mean he wanted to study?" Dad asked.

"Well, kind of," Bonnie said. "It wasn't homework, though. He'd dropped out of school; his family couldn't afford the fees."

"There was a famine in Malawi," Bonnie went on, "and they'd had to use their savings to buy food."

"Oh dear," said Mum. "You just don't realise how well off you really are, do you? I mean, we're just about to go and buy all the things for Christmas dinner, no problem at all. We don't have to think twice about buying a turkey and ham and popping them in the freezer, and there are people in Africa who don't have anything to eat."

We all thought about that. It was hard to imagine not having enough to eat, I thought. I mean, I might open the fridge and complain, "There's nothing to eat!", but what I'd really mean was, my favourite snack wasn't there. There was always, always something to eat.

"I'd like to read that book when you've finished it, Bonnie," Ted said. "This William Kamkwamba sounds like a really bright lad."

"Oh, he is!" said Bonnie. "He made electric lights for his family's home and then he made a water pump so they could get water out of a well to their veggie garden, even if there was a drought."

"How did he find out how to do it?" Elliot asked. "Especially if he wasn't at school any more?"

"He borrowed books from a library," Bonnie said. "That was why he decided to try to make lights, so he could read the books at night. And he even had to make his own tools, out of stuff from a junk heap."

"No Ted's shed to call on, eh?" said Dad. He looked at his watch. "We'd better get going," he said to Mum, "if we're going to the supermarket. It'll take a while seeing we're shopping up big for Christmas dinner. I don't want to miss getting just the right ham to do my special pineapple and ginger glaze on."

"Are you guys all right?" Mum said to Elliot and Bonnie and me. "How about I bring home pizza for dinner?"

"We're fine," we said. "Extra pepperoni, okay?"

When Mum and Dad had gone, I started to work on a new song on my guitar. Elliot, Bonnie and Ted took the pieces of the Power Up! kit out of the box and read the instructions again.

But although I was practising my new song, I was thinking about William Kamkwamba. I wasn't that keen on school, I didn't mind it, but it was just a place you had to go. I wondered how it would feel if you were told you couldn't go because your family couldn't pay the fees, and that was the end of it. It wouldn't feel good, I decided.

Chapter 6

Electric wind

That night, before I went to bed, I noticed *The Boy Who Harnessed the Wind* was lying on the table on the deck, beside the Power Up! kit. I picked it up. I read the blurb on the back. I read the inside jacket flap. Then I took the book off to my room and read a bit more. At midnight, I was still reading.

The book was about a 14-year-old boy who made what he called, in his language, *magetsi a mphepo* – electric wind.

His neighbours, and even his own family, thought he was crazy. Well, no wonder,

I thought, as I read. He built a five-metre tall, rickety tower out of bluegum wood in his family's back yard. It was so unstable that it swayed when the wind blew hard. On the top was a bicycle wheel and fan blades made from melted and flattened PVC piping.

William, I thought, I'd agree with your neighbours. I'd say you were *misala* (crazy), too.

But one afternoon, word went out around the village that William Kamkwamba was going to try something out, and everyone gathered to watch.

William, I read, started to climb the swaying, shaking tower. At the top, he connected two wires that were attached to a small light bulb he'd taken from a bicycle lamp. The fan blades weren't turning, a wire was holding them still. William released the wire and the blades began to turn in the wind. The tower shook and rocked as the wind blew harder, and William clung to it so he wouldn't be flung off.

The crowd, I read, couldn't work out what was going on. Why didn't this crazy boy come down? It was dangerous! What was he doing, hanging on there and staring at a little light bulb? Then … the bulb lit up. Everyone gasped. The power of the wind had produced electricity. And a 14-year-old boy had made it happen.

My eyes kept blinking and closing, but I couldn't stop reading. What was going to happen next?

Well, what happened next was that Mum saw my light was still on at midnight and she came in and very firmly turned it off. "What are you thinking, Xander? You've got school tomorrow! Go to sleep!"

So I went to sleep.

But my dreams were of me trying to persuade William Kamkwamba to build a tower and make electricity so I could play an electric guitar.

Bonnie put her Power up! kit together the next weekend. Ted was interested, so he kept calling in to see how things were going. Elliot kept wandering over to check it out, too. Our deck had more traffic than the main street of town at midday. Mind you, I was also keeping an eye on developments,. After reading William Kamkwamba's book, I wanted to see what the kit did, too.

They put together the pieces of a small windmill with four blades, on a solid base. They attached a little electric motor. They connected plastic-coated wires with little clips on the ends to a small light bulb. They attached a thing they called a multimeter that, apparently, measured volts – the amount of electricity flowing through a circuit – and the current, or amps, produced.

This all sounded like Swahili to me – or maybe Chichewa, which is what they speak in Malawi – but I supposed they knew what they were talking about.

It took a while to put it all together, but finally, "Done!" said Bonnie triumphantly.

"Time to test, then," said Elliot.

That's when they hit a problem. It was a still, grey day, the kind of day we often get in summer just before heavy rain comes. The sky was low, the air had a thick, hushed, waiting kind of feeling to it. There wasn't a whisper of wind. And that's not good when you want to test a windmill.

"Now what do we do?" Bonnie grumbled.

"Wait for wind, I guess," said Elliot.

"But I want to see if it works *now*," Bonnie wailed.

I stopped trying out my new song. "Try a fan," I said.

Bonnie, Elliot and Ted turned and looked at me.

"An electric fan," I said. "Put an electric fan in front of it."

"You know, Xander," said Elliot. "Sometimes you surprise me."

"Huh," I said. "I'm not just a pretty face, you know."

There was plenty of opportunity there for cheap shots, but Elliot and Bonnie let it go. Bonnie went off and came back with the biggest fan we had, and set it up. They put the little windmill in front of it and checked everything was connected properly.

"Ready?" said Bonnie. "Let's go!" She switched the fan on.

And the first thing that happened was that the windmill was blown straight over.

"The base isn't heavy enough," Ted said.

"So how can we make it heavier?" Bonnie worried. "Screw it to something heavier? Clamp it to the table?"

"Put a couple of bricks on it," I said.

Everyone turned and looked at me again.

"Honestly," I said. "You scientific types never go for the simplest solution."

Elliot found a couple of bricks and used them to weigh down the base.

Then Bonnie turned the fan on again. This time the windmill stayed in place. The blades spun. Elliot leaned eagerly over the multimeter. "It's happening!" he shouted.

"I'll attach the clips then!" Bonnie said. Her voice was shaking with excitement. "Okay, completing the circuit … now!"

We all watched the bulb. Nothing happened for a moment, then a faint, faint glow appeared.

"It's working, it's working!" Bonnie shrieked.

But the bulb just glowed dully.

"Why isn't it lighting up?" Bonnie moaned.

Ted checked the digital multimeter. "Right," he said. "The turbine's producing less than 1.5 volts. We need more than that to light up the bulb."

"How are you going to do that?" I asked.

"More wind," said Ted. "Bonnie, turn the fan up higher."

Bonnie did. The windmill blades spun faster. And the bulb lit up.

"We did it! We did it!" Bonnie leapt about. "We made electricity!"

"Just like William Kamkwamba," I said.

And again, they all stopped and looked at me. "What?" I said.

"That's quite an idea, Xander," said Ted.

"An idea?" I said. I didn't even know I'd had an idea.

Bonnie, Elliot and Ted were in a huddle. "Could we? Could we do it? Could we build a real windmill, a proper big one like William Kamkwamba did, and make electricity from it?"

I didn't get it. "Why would you want to do that? We have electricity! Why would you want to make more?"

Ted looked at me kindly. "Because we can, Xander," he said. "Just because we can."

Chapter 7

No power outage!

They started next day. It was a good day for it, because the grey, sultry, waiting kind of weather had turned to heavy rain.

Bonnie, Elliot and Ted disappeared into Ted's shed. They were there all day. When Mum asked me to go and get Elliot and Bonnie for dinner, I walked into the shed to find all kinds of weird junk spread out on the ground. An old electric ceiling fan, a bike wheel, part of a bike frame with the dynamo still attached to it, bits of wire, a couple of old car batteries, a very long old television aerial.

"Wow," I said. "Having a clear out?"

Bonnie gave me a look. "That's all the parts of our wind turbine," she said. "Tomorrow, we're putting them together."

"And the best of luck," I said. "Looks like a lot of old junk to me." But then I remembered. That's what they'd said about William Kamkwamba's windmill too.

The rain got even heavier as we were having dinner that night. Dad listened to it. "The bridge'll go under if this keeps up," he said. "If it does, we could be cut off over Christmas. Have we got everything we need?"

"All the food's in the freezer," said Mum comfortably. "Everyone finished their Christmas shopping?"

No one looked suddenly panicked, so it seemed as if we had.

"No worries, then," Mum said. "Let it rain!"

And it did. It rained all the next day and the next. Bonnie, Elliot and Ted spent all their time in Ted's shed. I checked on them occasionally, and found they'd managed to attach the bicycle wheel and its dynamo behind the blades of the fan. They'd made the blades longer by attaching extra pieces of plastic to them, cut to size. "The longer the blades, the more power we'll generate," Bonnie said.

They'd mounted the whole thing on the top of the old television aerial. "When we get it up, it'll need more bracing to make it secure," Ted said.

"But what are the car batteries for?" I wanted to know.

"Well, if the wind stops, the power stops too," Bonnie said. "But if we store it in a battery, we can still use it."

"Use it for what?"

"To power something in the house," Bonnie said. "Of course there's a problem …"

"And what's that?" I knew I'd be sorry I asked, and I was.

I got an earful. All about DC, or direct current, and AC, or alternating current, and how they'd have to convert the DC from the battery into AC to power some kind of appliance.

"And that means?" I asked.

"It means we need an inverter to convert DC to AC," said Ted.

"Oh, of course," I said. "Why didn't you just say?"

They all grinned at me.

Christmas was only four days away. The rain had stopped, but the creek was running swiftly and the bridge was well under. We could be cut off for a week or more. But it was all right, there was plenty of food.

Well, it was all right until the power went off. One minute we were having dinner, the next we were sitting in the dark.

"Drat!" said Mum, getting up and looking out the window. "The neighbours' lights are all off too. It's not just us, then."

"It'll come on again soon," Dad said.

But it didn't. We had no power that night, and none the next day. We could cope, we had candles and we could cook on the gas barbecue on the deck. But by the end of that day, Mum was looking worried. "There's all the food in the freezer," she said. "If we don't open the door, it'll be all right until maybe tomorrow. After that – well, I wouldn't like to risk it."

Then she looked even more worried. "We've got plenty of canned food, but unless the power comes back on, it might be baked beans for Christmas dinner."

"No turkey?" said Elliot. "No ham?"

"Not if the freezer stays off," said Mum.

"But if the freezer was working it'd be okay?" said Bonnie.

"Well, yes," said Mum. "But the freezer's not going to work without power."

Bonnie and Elliot looked at each other, got up and rushed out.

"Where are you going?" Mum called.

"To see Ted!" they called back. They didn't come back for a long time.

Chapter 8

A very different Christmas

When Bonnie and Elliot came back, they were looking for muscle.

"We need to get the aerial up and brace it," Ted explained to Dad. "It'll go up the side of your deck all right, but we'll need to brace it to the roof. Is that all right?"

Dad thought about it. "Is it going to take the roof off when the wind blows harder than it is now?" he asked.

Ted thought about that for a minute. "Well, probably not. We'll make sure we brace it to the roof really tight so it doesn't," he said.

Dad looked at Bonnie, dancing around in excitement. "We'll give it a go, then," he said.

Ted and Elliot rounded up all the neighbours who could climb a ladder or hammer a nail in straight. They carried the television aerial and its braces out of the shed.

"Tell me again what this is going to do?" Mr Harper said.

"It's going to run our freezer," Bonnie said. "We think."

"You might need bigger batteries than those car ones for that," Mr Harper said. "How about a boat battery? Or something from a tractor?"

"Good thinking," Ted said. "But let's get this up first."

By the end of the afternoon, the aerial was up. Dad and Ted and Elliot crawled all over the roof, fixing the bracing in place.

"Seems sturdy enough," Ted said at last. "Now we need the fan and bike up here. Right, mates, this is where we need the muscle."

We pulled the windmill up with a rope and pulley, and Ted had been right, it did take a lot of muscle. "Elliot," he called, just before we started pulling, "make sure those blades are tied down. If we get it up and it starts turning, we'll never stop it."

We heaved, and we tugged, and we heaved some more. The fan slowly rose into the air, beside the television aerial. Ted, at the top, bolted it into place.

"Right, Bonnie," he called down. "Big moment. Will I let it rip? Have you got the test bulb ready?"

Bonnie nodded.

"Here goes then." Ted connected the wires. He came down the ladder as far as he could and released the wires that were holding the blades still. The blades began to turn.

They turned faster and faster. The aerial and the braces vibrated. The roof shook a little.

"Cripes!" said Ted. He climbed down quickly, holding tightly to the ladder. "That seems to be working all right. A bit more than I expected, actually. How's the bulb, Bonnie?"

Bonnie didn't answer. I looked at her. Her eyes were shut tight. "I can't look," she said.

"Bonnie," I said. "You can look now. The bulb's lit up. It's working."

The windmill was producing electricity, but there was still work to be done before it could run the freezer. Our freezer wasn't huge, but it needed power stored in batteries to keep it running all the time. But, by late in the afternoon, Ted had connected it. We all held our breaths and listened. And there it was – a click and a hum as the freezer came on. We all cheered.

"Right," said Mum. "Elliot, Xander, run over to the neighbours and tell them our freezer's going, and ask if they need to store some food in it. Oh, and tell them to pray for the wind to keep up, too! Just in case the mains power doesn't come on again."

The mains power didn't come on again until after Christmas. But it didn't matter by then. The windmill kept our freezer going.

On Christmas Eve, all the neighbours came to get their food out of our freezer. Then something hit them. "The food is fine," said Mrs Wong. "But my stove's still not working!"

"Nor is ours," said Mrs Singh.

"I thought of that," Mum said. "What about we all share? We've got the gas barbecue on the deck. It'll work, I'm sure."

So we had a very different Christmas that year. All of us, and all the neighbours, on our deck. We had barbecued turkey pieces, barbecued ham slices, potatoes fried on the barbecue, even Christmas pudding boiled up in a big saucepan of water on the barbecue. Mrs Wong made spicy plum sauce, and Mrs Singh made some curry sauces.

"You know, we don't really celebrate Christmas," said Mrs Singh. "But I'm not going to miss a good party!"

There was plenty to eat.

"That was absolutely splendid!" Ted declared. He raised his glass. "To Bonnie's brilliant windmill!"

"Oh, no," said Bonnie. "To all the incredible junk in Ted's shed!"

"To everyone for helping to build the windmill," Dad said.

"To William Kamkwamba for the idea!" I said.

So we drank a toast to all of that, and then I brought my guitar out, and Mum and Dad got their fiddle and flute, and we all sang for the rest of the afternoon. Above us, the roof quivered and vibrated as the blades of my geeky sister's science project spun in the sky.